Helping Children See Jesus

ISBN: 978-1-64104-059-4

Christ, the Head of the Church
New Testament Volume 31:
Colossians

Author: R. Iona Lyster
Illustrator: Frances H. Hertzler
Colorization courtesy of Good Life Ministries
Page Layout: Patricia Pope

© 2019 Bible Visuals International
PO Box 153, Akron, PA 17501-0153
Phone: (717) 859-1131
www.biblevisuals.org

All rights reserved. No part of this publication may be reproduced, stored in a retrieval system or transmitted in any form by any means, electronic, mechanical, photocopy, recording or otherwise, without the prior permission of the publisher, except as provided by USA copyright law.

RELATED ITEMS

To access related items (such as activities, memory verse posters and translated texts) please visit our web store at www.biblevisuals.org and enter 1031 in the search box on the page.

FREE TEXT DOWNLOAD

To access a FREE printable copy of the teaching text (PDF format) in English or other available languages, enter S1031DL in the search box. Add the item to your cart, and use coupon code XTACSV17 at checkout. Once your order is processed you will receive an email with a link to the free download.

STUDENT ACTIVITES

These are included with the FREE printable copy of the English teaching text for this story. See the directions under Free Text Download (above) to access them.

A

C

B

- 6 -

That in all things Christ might have the preeminence.

Colossians 1:18b

Lesson 1
CHRIST: HIGH OVER ALL

NOTE TO THE TEACHER

The city of Colosse was in Phrygia, a district in Asia Minor. Paul worked in that region for three years. (See Acts 20:31.) On Illustration #1 the background is a map of the area of Phrygia. It is marked: *. Colosse has this mark: #. Ephesus is marked: +. You may want to print these place names on the map and refer to them when teaching.

From Colossians 1:7 and 4:12-13, it appears that Epaphras probably started the church at Colosse and became its first pastor. When he went to Rome to see Paul, it would seem (from Colossians 4:17 and Philemon 1-2) that Archippus (probably Philemon's son) served as interim pastor. Like many other churches of that day, it met in a home, probably Philemon's. (See Philemon 1-2.)

Remember this: The Christians who made up the first churches came from various backgrounds. Some had been pagan idol worshipers, while some knew the Jewish religion. If Paul or one of the other apostles could not be present, men of lesser abilities did the teaching. Because the New Testament was not yet completed, the Christians lacked written guidance. As a result, problems arose. It was so in Colosse.

It may have been for this reason that Pastor Epaphras went to Rome 700 miles away. There he became (perhaps voluntarily) a prisoner with the Apostle Paul. (See Philemon 23.) From Paul he learned the solutions to the Colossian problems. Epaphras, we are told, was a faithful minister of Christ who prayed fervently for the Colossians. (See Colossians 1:7; 4:12.)

The problem in the church at Colosse was this: A false teaching had come in which insisted that because man is so sinful and God is so holy (which is true) the sinner had to approach Him through many angelic beings (which is not true). These beings were go-betweens from man to God. By accepting this incorrect teaching, the Colossians were ignoring our Lord as the only One to go between man and God. (See 1 Timothy 2:5-6; Hebrews 7:25; 1 John 2:1.) This false system included the worship of angels and strict self-denial. (See 2:18, 20-22.) Such teaching later became known as Gnosticism, meaning (in the Greek language) knowledge. The Gnostics claimed to possess secret knowledge and wisdom.

The Holy Spirit, overseeing Paul's writing, answered all these wrong ideas. (An understanding of Colossians is much needed today. Unfortunately, there are many who are deceived as those in Colosse were.) In this epistle we learn that all the fullness of God is in Christ alone. (See Colossians 1:19; 2:9.)

Those who trust in Christ have full knowledge and wisdom. (See 2:2-3. Read also 1:9-10, 28; 3:10, 16.) Further, Christ is shown to be the solution to all that mystified the false teachers. (See 1:26-27. The word *mystery* appears also in 2:2 and 4:3.) Because Jesus is who He is and what He is, He is the Head–the Head of the universe and the Head of the body of Christian believers, the Church. (See 1:18; 2:10, 19; compare Ephesians 1:22-23; 4:15-16.) Christ's Headship is the subject of this volume.

Scripture to be studied: Colossians 1; Acts 19:1-41

The *aim* of the lesson: To show that because Christ is high over all, we should give Him first place in our lives.

What your students should *know*: That God has placed Christ over everything.

What your students should *feel*: Humbled, that One so lofty would live within them.

What your students should *do*: Examine their lives and unload those things which have kept Christ from having first place.

Lesson outline (for the teacher's and students' notebooks):
1. Beginnings of the Colossian church (1:1-8).
2. Colossian problems and Paul's prayer (1:9-11).
3. Christ, Lord of all (1:17-23).
4. Christ in the believer (1:24-29).

The verse to be memorized:

That in all things Christ might have the preeminence.
(Colossians 1:18b)

THE LESSON

The Apostle Paul was an energetic missionary. He traveled widely, introducing people to the Lord Jesus, preaching the Gospel, teaching new converts, starting churches. Occasionally he hurried from one place to another. At other times he remained for long periods. When he was in Phrygia (the region in which the city of Colosse was located), he stayed for three years. Two of those years he spent in the city of Ephesus. (See Acts 19:10.) People from all over Asia came to hear him tell of the Lord Jesus. What crowds he must have preached to! Among those who heard the Good News there could have been some from Colosse. While we have no record of exactly what happened, we believe it may have been like this: Word reached Colosse that Paul was preaching a new message–a message from God. Epaphras, Philemon, and Archippus wanted to hear what Paul had to say. So, after packing a few things, they headed for Ephesus more than 100 miles away.

Day after day they plodded along under the hot sun. Often they asked each other, "What has changed Paul? Everyone says he used to hate Christians. Now he himself is one. And he's not quiet about it! Everywhere he goes, he preaches about Christ. Whatever happened to him?" The three were puzzled. In Ephesus it was a simple matter to find Paul. Everyone knew him or so it seemed to the three from Colosse. Even the idol-makers' could tell where to find him. Earnestly the men listened to Paul's preaching. Soon it became clear to them that this was truly a message from God. They were convinced that the Lord Jesus Christ is God's Son. They received Him as Saviour and turned their backs on their old, sinful lives. Eagerly they received everything Paul taught them about their new faith in Christ.

All the way home the three made fervent plans to tell the Gospel in their city. They amazed themselves for they, too, were completely changed. Their old superstitious pagan religion could never again satisfy them. Having turned to the Saviour, their lives were gloriously new.

1. BEGINNINGS OF THE COLOSSIAN CHURCH
Colossians 1:1-8

When they arrived home, the men immediately announced that meetings would be held at Philemon's house.

Show Illustration #1

The Colossians were always curious to hear anything new. So they came. They listened attentively and liked what they heard! Before long several believed in Christ and received Him as Saviour. Then it was decided that they must have a church. Philemon said they could have it in his home. (See Philemon 1-2.) So that is where it was. And Epaphras was the minister. (See Colossians 1:7.)

Things went well with the new Christians in Colosse. Right from the start their lives were changed. They loved each other (1:4, 8). They had joy and peace. They were gentle and good. (See 1:6; compare John 15:16; Galatians 5:22-23; Philippians 1:11.) Their days were very happy.

2. COLOSSIAN PROBLEMS AND PAUL'S PRAYER
Colossians 1:9-11

Then something happened. New teachers boasting of their knowledge came to the church. The Colossians listened, because they liked to learn new things.

The teachers spoke of God's holiness. They discussed the wickedness of sin that separated man from God. On and on they continued, explaining the vast difference between God the holy One, and sinful people. The Colossians agreed wholeheartedly.

Then the leading teacher, looking quite wise declared, "You Colossians think that because you believe in Christ, God will accept you." The Colossians nodded in agreement. Puffing himself up, he continued, "To us who have studied the secrets of the universe, it seems that since man and God are so far apart, there need to be many stepping-stones to Him. Christ is one stepping-stone, but only one. In our opinion there are many spirit-beings and angels who go between us and God."

Show Illustration #2

"We think they are also worthy of worship. So we pray to them." (See 2:18.) The new teachers had other ideas, too. They felt that the angels did a lot of work and said many prayers for each person. "To be worthy of the angels' work and prayers," they said, "you Colossians must do as we do: refuse to taste or touch certain things. (See 2:21.) You must follow some of the Jewish laws if you want God to accept you." One said, "There are certain kinds of meat you dare not eat." Another insisted, "You have to observe Jewish holy days and the Sabbath." (See 2:16.)

The teachers spoke as if they had great authority. They challenged the Colossians to do some thinking as they themselves had done. "We are scientists of the mind [philosophers]," they declared. (See Colossians 2:8.)

These men were so convincing that the poor Colossians began to accept their false teaching. What a mixed-up group they became! Instead of worshiping the Lord Jesus Christ and Him alone, they prayed to angels. They practiced self-denial. Even though they were not Jews, they studied the Jewish law. As a result, they would not eat certain meats. They observed the Jewish holy days and Sabbaths. They wanted to be worthy of their salvation, and wanted to remain saved. If it meant doing these things, they would do them!

Philemon, Epaphras and Archippus knew the men were not teaching truth, But how could they prove it? They didn't have the education these worldly wise teachers had. They couldn't persuade the Colossians that their new practices were wrong.

There was only one thing to do. One of them would have to go to see the Apostle Paul. He would have the answers. It would be a long, tiresome journey. For by this time Paul was a prisoner in Rome 700 miles away! It was agreed that Epaphras would go and Archippus would remain in charge. (See Colossians 4:17.)

Weeks later Epaphras got to Rome. He found that to spend time with Paul, he would have to stay in prison with him. And this is exactly what he did. (See Philemon 23.) When Paul learned what had happened in Colosse, he immediately began to pray for the Christians there. (See 1:9.) Then he wrote to them and sent the letter with two men, Tychicus and Onesimus. (See 4:7-9; compare Ephesians 6:21-22; Philemon 9-19.)

It was a happy day in Colosse when Paul's letter was delivered. Many in the church had never seen Paul. (See 2:1.) So it was a special treat to have a message directly from him. When Paul spoke of the Colossians' Christian love and of their doing good (see 1:4, 6, 8), they beamed. (*Teacher:* Depending upon the age of your class, you may want to read verses 1-8.)

It pleased them that Paul should pray for the very things they desired: knowledge and wisdom. It was perfectly clear, however, that he wasn't speaking of the false "knowledge" and wisdom of the proud new teachers. Paul wrote, "I pray . . . that you might be filled with the super knowledge . . . of God. I pray God will give you every kind of wisdom [to use knowledge correctly] and understanding which comes from Him. I pray that you will increase in your knowledge of God." (See 1:9-11.)

3. CHRIST, LORD OF ALL
Colossians 1:12-23

Show Illustration #3

The letter continued, "God has fitted us for His kingdom of light. God rescued us out of the fearsome kingdom of Satan's darkness and put us into the kingdom of the Son of His love." (*Teacher:* Point to darkness and light in illustration.) "God did this because Christ paid for our sins with His blood." (*Teacher:* Point to cross. You may want to read verses 12-14.)

One of the church leaders jumped up and exclaimed, "He doesn't mention the angels. It sounds as if God accepts us because of Christ alone. What else does he say?" The man reading the letter answered, "He mentions a number of things about Christ." (*Teacher:* Have your students list these in their notebooks.)

1. Christ has made God known to us (1:15a; compare John 1:18; 14:9-11).
2. Christ has first place in the universe, for He created everything in the heavens and upon the earth (1:15b-16; compare John 1:3; Hebrews 1:2). (*Teacher:* In illustration, point to hand creating globe.)
3. Christ was before all things were made and He holds everything together (1:17).
4. Christ is the head of His body, the church (1:18a). ("The church" means all who have put their trust in Christ.)
5. Christ is Lord over all because He rose from the dead. He has first place now and forever (1:18b).
6. Christ is God–God in limitless fullness! (1:19).
7. Christ, by His death changed [reconciled] us whose, trust is in Him (1:20).

Now, instead of being wicked sinners far from God, we are changed so that when we stand before Him, no sin will be charged against us. (Compare Ephesians 2:13; Romans 5:10-

11; 2 Corinthians 5:19-21.) Surely the Colossians began to see that the know-it-all teachers were wrong when they said Christ is one of many stepping-stones to God. He is the only One who can bring us to God! (See 1 Peter 3:18.)

4. CHRIST IN THE BELIEVER
Colossians 1:24-29

The reading of the letter continued, and when the Colossians heard the word "mystery" they pricked up their ears. (The new teachers had freely talked about their study of mysterious things.) "God has now shown a mystery which has been His secret forever. This is it: Christ is in you." (See 1:26-27; compare Galatians 2:20.)

Show Illustration #4

Now God's secret is known; so it is no longer a secret! The Lord Jesus Christ, the One high over all, lived in the Colossian Christians. And if He is your Saviour, He lives in you. Because He lives in you now, some day you will live with Him in His glorious Heaven-home. Until then, will you give Him first place in every part of your life? If you do this, God Himself will fill you. (See Ephesians 3:1-19.) Then you will be a sparkling Christian, bubbling with joy, peace and love. (See John 7:38; compare Isaiah 58:11.)

(*Teacher:* Suggest some ways in which Christians in your area push Christ out of first place. Encourage your students to discuss why these things keep Christ from having first place and what should be done to correct them. Each one should list in his/her notebook what is wrong in his/her own life. Allow time for silent confession to God. He will doubtless reveal solutions to their problems, things which they can do to correct those problems today or this week. These, too, should be written in their notebooks, before you close with prayer.)

Give opportunity to the unsaved to receive the Saviour.

Lesson 2
THE FULLNESS OF GOD IN CHRIST

NOTE TO THE TEACHER

Creative Bible Teaching is a helpful book for every teacher. (Author: Lawrence O. Richards. Published by Moody Press, Chicago, IL.) We trust it is (or will be) in your church library and that you will refer to it often.

In that book, the author shows that Paul's prayer for the Colossians (1:9b-11) is a pattern for the kind of teaching which will produce results:

1. "That you might be filled with the knowledge of that which God has willed." Teach so carefully that your students will have a knowledge of God's Word. Only then will they grow spiritually, learning "what the will of the Lord is" for them personally (Ephesians 5:17).
2. "In all wisdom and spiritual understanding." Wisdom enables a person to recognize a proper course of action. Understanding is the ability to see clearly into the true nature of things. Guide your students, therefore, to relate Bible knowledge to daily living.
3. "That you may walk in a manner worthy of the Lord, to please Him utterly!" Your students must respond to Bible knowledge by living lives that please the Lord. It is your duty, teacher, to show them how to respond.
4. "Bearing fruit in every good work." When a person knows God's Word, understands it and responds to it, He will be a fruitful Christian. (See Galatians 5:22-23.)
5. "And increasing in the knowledge of God." God will continually reveal new truths to those who respond to Him. (See John 14:21.)

If you will pray for your students as Paul prayed for the Colossians and teach accordingly, you'll see them grow spiritually.

Ask yourself: Is my teaching producing spiritual results? Are my students growing in grace? (See 2 Peter 3:18.)

The many Scripture references in these lessons are for your own guidance, teacher. Do not overload your students by using them in class.

Scripture to be studied: Colossians 2:1-12

The *aim* of the lesson: To show that believers are joined to Christ when their trust is in Him.

What your students should *know*: Because Christ is the Head and believers are His body, whatever is true of the Head is true of the body.

What your students should *feel*: A hatred for anything that pushes Christ out of first place.

What your saved students should *do*: Acknowledge their union with Christ by being baptized.

Lesson outline (for the teacher's and students' notebooks):
1. True wisdom and knowledge are in Christ (2:1-7).
2. Christ is God in all His fullness (2:8-9).
3. Christian believers have fullness in Christ (2:10).
4. Christian believers have resurrection life (2:11-12).

The verse to be memorized:

That in all things Christ might have the preeminence.
(Colossians 1:18b)

THE LESSON

Let us suppose that a new kind of food has been produced. You are told that by eating it every day you will be exceptionally wise and have superior knowledge. Would you rush to the market to get that food? Yes, of course. Why? Suppose it was expensive? (*Teacher:* Encourage your class to discuss this.)

Almost all of us want to be wise. We enjoy investigating things and knowing all the answers. We would be quite pleased to hear someone say of us, "Ask him/her whatever you want to know; he/she knows everything!"

The people who lived in Colosse long ago were much like us. They wanted to be wise; they liked to learn anything new. That is why they were deceived by the big-sounding talk of the visiting teachers.

1. TRUE WISDOM AND KNOWLEDGE ARE IN CHRIST
Colossians 2:17

When Paul wrote to the Colossians, he spoke of his deep concern for them. There in jail he was continually praying for them so earnestly and vigorously, he said that it took all his strength. (See 2:1.) Surely the Christians in Colosse had a jolt when they heard from Paul's letter: "All the wealth of wisdom and knowledge are in Christ. Don't be led astray by the high-sounding nonsense which men have dreamed up." (See 1:27; 2:2-4.)

One of the church leaders doubtless spoke up saying, "Because those new teachers said they had studied mysteries [of the universe] we believed them. We accepted their idea that Christ is only one of many stepping-stones to God, We were wrong! We must never again listen to anyone who puts others on an equal level with the Lord Jesus Christ. God has placed Him high above all. It is our responsibility to give Him His rightful place. Then, instead of having the knowledge of these new teachers, we shall have God's full knowledge." The others agreed enthusiastically.

Show Illustration #5

They settled back to hear more of Paul's letter. "You have placed your trust in Christ Jesus the Lord. So let Him, the Lord, control your life. You have been rooted in Him." (*Teacher:* Point to roots in illustration.) The Colossians understood this perfectly.

They knew that trees get life from their roots. So they who had received Christ got their life, their wisdom, their knowledge from Him, not from man-made ideas.

"Keep on being built up in Christ," Paul added. (*Teacher:* Point to building in illustration.) This, too, was clear to the Christians in Colosse. They knew that if a building is to be strong, it must have a good, solid foundation, A house built on sand will collapse in a severe storm or flood. Just so, the person who accepts what men think, or suppose, has a shaky foundation. Our complete trust must be in Christ alone. (See John 14:6; 1 Corinthians 3:11; compare Ephesians 3:17-19.) He who is the Head of the universe (because He created it) and the Head of the body of believers (because He bought them with His blood) is also the Christian's foundation. (*Teacher:* Read 1 Corinthians 3:11 to your class.) We know this is true because God's Word teaches it. (Do you see the scroll in the illustration? Remember, God's Word was once written on scrolls.)

2. CHRIST IS GOD IN ALL HIS FULLNESS
Colossians 2:8-9

The Christians in Colosse paid strict attention when Paul warned them: "Be on guard! Do not fall into the trap of those teachers who guess and imagine certain things are so." (*Teacher:* Observe also the warnings in 2:4, 18.)

Paul knew how often the new teachers proudly used the word *fullness.* Their ideas, their thoughts, and their knowledge were *fullness,* so they said. Also, according to them, although God was *fullness*–an immeasurable reservoir–Christ was only a tiny stream out of God's fullness.

The Holy Spirit guided Paul to write: "All the fullness of God lives ever and always in Christ." (Compare John 1:14; Colossians 1:19.)

Show Illustration #6a

Before the Lord Jesus came to earth, even before the world was made—Christ was God in His fullness! (See John 1:14; 17:5; Philippians 2:6; Colossians 1:19.)

Show Illustration 6b

That fullness of God lived in the body and life of a man when Christ came down to live on earth. (See John 5:18; 10:30.)

Show Illustration 6c

Now He is back in Heaven with the Father and, as always, is God in His fullness. (See 1 Timothy 3:16.)

After hearing this, you may be certain the Colossians would have discussed it for some time. They agreed: "Since Christ is everything that God is, He is certainly far above angels and spirit beings. So it is not necessary to worship them. Indeed, to worship angels and spirit beings is sin!" (See 1 Timothy 2:5.)

3. CHRISTIAN BELIEVERS HAVE FULLNESS IN CHRIST
Colossians 2:10

The Colossians snapped back to attention when they heard from the letter: "You who have placed your trust in Christ are complete in Him." They knew that *complete* meant filled full. Christians are filled full of Christ! Because they, His body, are joined to Him, the Head, His life is filling them continually. (See John 1:16; compare Ephesians 3:17-19.)

Show Illustration #7

The Colossians understood this because they undoubtedly got their water from a well. Some went in the early morning. Others may have gone later in the day. Day after day they drew one pitcherful after another from the well. Every person and all the animals always had plenty of water. Yet, no matter how much water was used, the well was continually full. Its fullness came from a never-ending river deep in the heart of the earth.

Just so, anyone who opens his/her heart and life to Christ has His everlasting fullness. (See John 4:14; compare 1 Corinthians 3:23.) And that fullness includes His wisdom. (See 1 Corinthians 1:30.)

Do you think the Colossians had some questions? Surely one who had to work hard in school wanted to know: "If wisdom and knowledge are in Christ and I, because I am a Christian, have His fullness, why should I study so hard? I have everything I need when I belong to Christ. Isn't it enough just to think about God and Christ instead of studying other things?" (*Teacher:* Allow your students to discuss this.)

That would have been an easy question for the Apostle Paul to answer. He was one of the best educated men of his day. He knew from his own experience that God used his persevering study. He was therefore able to speak intelligently to the wisest people in many lands. He could write letters that taught great truths of God to those who lived long ago, letters (like Colossians) which teach us today. On many of his missionary journeys, Paul had with him a doctor, Luke, who had also studied diligently in order to become a good physician.

God never says that Christians should not study. He does not praise ignorance. He does say, "The fear of the Lord is the beginning of wisdom" (Proverbs 9:10). And "Study to show yourself approved unto God, a workman that needeth not to be ashamed, rightly dividing the word of truth" (2 Timothy 2:15). So, while He encourages us to get wisdom and understanding (Proverbs 4:5-7), these are to be kept in their right places.

The Lord Jesus Christ is to have first place always. Anything is wrong that pushes Him into a small part of the Christian's life. God has made Him Head of the universe, Head of the body of believers, and Head of all the angels and spirit beings. (See Colossians 1:16; 2:10b; 1 Peter 3:22.) The believer's responsibility is to do as God has done: give Him the highest place.

4. CHRISTIAN BELIEVERS HAVE RESURRECTION LIFE
Colossians 2:11-12

Were there any in the Colossian church who thought of the Lord Jesus only as a great teacher or a perfect example? The Holy Spirit reminded them that Christ is much more than a teacher or example. He is the Saviour. (See Colossians 2:11-12.)

He, God the Son, took upon Himself the sins of us all–and the punishment for those sins–when He died on the cross. (See Isaiah 53:6; Romans 6:23; 1 Peter 2:24.) Although He was buried, He did not–could not–stay dead. Having paid for our sins, He arose and He lives forevermore, giving to those who receive Him His kind of life–eternal life. If a person's head is dead, is his body dead? (*Teacher:* Encourage student response to all of these questions.) If his head rises from the dead, does his body rise? If his head has life, does his body have life? Christ is the Head of the Church. Each believer is a part of the Church, which is His body. Is everything which is true of Christ the Head, true of those who are His body? Are the Head and body one? (See John 17:21.24.) Because Christ has risen from the dead, all who believe in Him have His life in them.

Show Illustration #8

How did the Colossian Christians prove that they were joined to Christ? By being baptized. (See Colossians 2:12; compare Romans 6:4; Matthew 28:19; Acts 2:41; 16:33; 18:8.)

One of Christ's last commands was that those who trust in Him are to be baptized. (See Matthew 28:19.) We please Him when we obey Him. When we obey Him, we acknowledge that He is our Head.

Have you been baptized? By going down into the water, you are saying: "I believe that Christ died and was buried for my sins. I am now turning my back on my old sinful life, counting it dead." Coming up out of the water, you are testifying, "I believe Christ proved He is God's Son by rising from the grave. Because I have trusted in Him, I am joined to Him. So I, too, have been raised and have Christ's life in me. He is my living Head." (*Teacher:* If any question the mode of baptism in the illustration, please show them Mark 1:9-10: Acts 8:36-39: Romans 6:3-5.)

Have you placed your trust in Christ? If so, have you been baptized, showing others that you are His?

If you have not received the Saviour, will you do so now?

(*Teacher:* If possible, you and your pastor should counsel the believers who have not been baptized.)

Lesson 3
CHRIST IS ALL-SUFFICIENT

NOTE TO THE TEACHER

Your born-again students should be giving serious thought to the matter of baptism, which was mentioned in the last lesson. If you have a majority who have not been baptized, discuss the subject in class, using Scripture to show its importance. If necessary, use *The Church* (New Testament Volume 15), and review the second lesson: "The Church: What It Does."

The memory verse for this volume helps us understand the book of Colossians. For the Christian, the one thing that counts is the position of Christ in one's life.

Remember: It is not our wisdom nor our religious thoughts, not our church activities nor sacrifices, not worship of angels, not neglecting or torturing our bodies, that pleases God. It is God's Son who pleases God. He is the One who saved us and brought us to God. He is to have first place in all that we do and are. This pleases God.

Does Christ have first place in your life, teacher? Do you stand up for Him when someone tells an impure joke? Does He have first place in your money habits? In your dress? In your home? In your life's goals? If so, you can enthusiastically encourage your students to give Him the preeminence.

You will have no trouble getting the simple objects mentioned in the third section of this lesson. This is taken from an excellent book entitled *Easy Object Lessons*.* We suggest that you obtain this book for you will use it often. The 60 lessons are applicable to all ages. The objects used are simple ones which you probably have at home.

If your people do not have television, change the first part of the lesson. Have the announcement made in the center of town (or wherever your people meet for important events).

* *Easy Object Lessons* by Dr. Charles C. Ryrie. Copyright 1970. Published by Moody Press, Chicago, IL. Used by permission.

Scripture to be studied: Colossians 2:13-3:4

The *aim* of the lesson: To show that nothing can be added to the salvation which Christ purchased for us with His blood.

What your students should *know*: By His death, Christ paid for our sins, cancelled dependence upon the old Jewish law, and keeps us safe forever.

What your students should *feel*: Amazement, that One so exalted would provide salvation for us, so lowly.

What your students should *do*: Check their motives for the good things they do. Are these done as an expression of thanks for their great salvation? Or have they been hoping that their good deeds would help to keep them saved?

Lesson outline (for the teacher's and students' notebooks):

1. Believers in Christ do not need to follow Jewish laws (2:13-17). (Nor does anyone need to follow them!)
2. Believers in Christ do not need to worship angels or punish themselves (2:18-23).
3. Believers in Christ are safe in Christ (3:1-3).
4. When Christ reigns on earth, His body of believers will reign with Him (3:4).

The verse to be memorized:

That in all things Christ might have the preeminence.
(Colossians 1:18b)

THE LESSON

Suppose you heard this TV announcement: "A letter of tremendous importance has come from _____. (**Teacher:** Name a prominent person: the president, perhaps, the king or queen, or a famous astronaut.) "It will be read tomorrow morning at 6:00 o'clock on this station."

Would people tune in? Would children listen? Yes, indeed! And they would be close to the set to see and hear everything.

When the Colossian Christians received their letter from the great Apostle Paul, everyone assembled and listened carefully to each word. Did everyone understand everything that was in the letter? They could because the same Holy Spirit who guided Paul as he wrote the letter also lived within the believers. So He helped them as He helps us to understand it.

Of course the children may have had some difficulty understanding. What did they do? Could it have been like this?

Archippus hurried home, clutching Paul's letter. His children jumped and ran, trying to keep up with his long strides. They tugged at him, begging, "What does it mean, Daddy? Please explain it to us."

"I will, I will," he assured them. "Mother is home caring for the baby; so I'll tell her and you at the same time."

As soon as the meal was cleared away, Archippus and his family did what most Christian families did then (and what many do today). They sang a hymn of praise to God, discussed God's Word and prayed together. (See Deuteronomy 6:6-9.) This time, however, Archippus held in his hands a totally new part of the Word of God: Paul's letter to the Colossians. (The New Testament which we now have was not complete at that time, and the books were not yet assembled. That was done later.)

Archippus read again what had been read to the assembly. Mother and children listened quietly, reverently and curiously. For Father had set before them an egg, a heavy pot and a hammer.

1. BELIEVERS IN CHRIST DO NOT NEED TO FOLLOW JEWISH LAWS
Colossians 2:13-17

He began, "When the new teachers came here to Colosse, they told us we had to obey the old Jewish law. They said that if we didn't do so, we couldn't be saved. The law which God gave to the Jews was holy. It was good. (See Romans 7:12.) It showed what sin is (Romans 3:20; 7:7) and told the punishment for sin. However, no one (except the Lord Jesus Christ) ever obeyed the law perfectly. Disobeying the law meant punishment.

"God is reminding us (through Brother Paul's letter) that when Christ gave himself on Calvary, He took the punishment for all our sins forever. (See Hebrews 10:12-14.) When we place our trust in Him, He forgives all our sins." (See 2:13.)

Show Illustration #9

Archippus continued, "Not only did Christ pay for our sins, but He also cancelled the old law. (See Romans 10:4; Galatians 3:23-25.) We have a custom to help us understand this. If I buy something but do not pay for it immediately, the man from whom I bought it nails a bill to our door. (**Teacher:** Point to bill on door.) Everyone who passes can see how much I owe and to whom I owe it. When I pay the money to him, he will cross out the bill. Then everyone will know it is paid. It's blotted out. There is nothing charged against me.

"Once a bill is paid, does it ever need to be paid again? No! But that is exactly what our people have been attempting to do. They think that if they follow parts of the old law, they themselves can pay for their sins. So they observe the Jewish holy days and Sabbaths. They refuse to eat certain meats. But the Holy Spirit tells us here in Paul's letter that Christ's death crossed out the old law–the bill that showed we were sinners. (Point to the cross over the tablets of the law.) (See Romans 8:3-4; Galatians 3:13, 24-25; 4:4, 5.) Because Jesus paid it all (Romans 8:1-2), is there anything more to be paid? Indeed not! Our salvation is perfect; it is complete. Nothing can be added."

Do you suppose Archippus' children had questions? Do you have any questions? (**Teacher:** Encourage class discussion. Don't proceed until your students have a clear understanding of the completeness of the substitutionary work of Christ.)

2. BELIEVERS IN CHRIST DO NOT NEED TO WORSHIP ANGELS OR PUNISH THEMSELVES
Colossians 2:18-23

Show Illustration #10

Archippus continued, "Because Paul wrote this letter to us, we know God's truth. The new teachers taught only their own ideas, and they were wrong. They said we have to worship angels. [Point to people worshiping angels.] They also insisted we couldn't eat certain foods even though they were perfectly harmless. [Point to people refusing food.] They commanded us to punish our bodies so we could make ourselves pure.

"Their big-sounding talk impressed many of our Colossian Christians. One of our leading men told me, 'I am so ignorant and unworthy that I dare not pray directly to God the Father. So I am worshiping angels and spirits who speak to God for me. They know better than I how to express my thoughts.'"

Archippus's voice rose in earnestness: "Such talk is sin! It makes a person sound as if he is taking a low place. Instead, he is proudly puffing up himself. He is saying he is wiser than God. God says there is only One who can go between him and man: the Lord Jesus Christ. (See 1 Timothy 2:5; 1 John 2:1; Hebrews 7:25.) So if we pray to angels, or spirits, or holy people, we're saying we don't believe what God says and that we know better than He does."

Archippus turned slowly from one to the other, studying each face. Solemnly he said, "Never, never forget this: when our trust is in the Lord Jesus Christ, we are joined to Him forever. We are His body; He is our Head. We can't do one thing to make ourselves pure and good. Going without certain foods or punishing our bodies will never make us acceptable to God. The Lord Jesus is the only One who can make us acceptable to God—either *before* or *after* we are saved. This is because he took the punishment for all our sins once for all and forever. [Point to cross in illustration.] Punishing ourselves means nothing."

3. BELIEVERS IN CHRIST ARE SAFE IN CHRIST
Colossians 3:1-3

"Daddy, what are you going to do with the egg, the pot and the hammer?" the youngest boy wanted to know.

"I'll show you right now," Archippus answered with a smile. "But first let's read Colossians 3:1-3." (*Teacher:* Read these verses, repeating verse 3.) "The Holy Spirit tells us through Paul's letter: 'Your life is hid with Christ in God.' We'll let this egg, which can be broken easily, represent a weak Christian—one who is always afraid he might lose his salvation.

(*Teacher:* Hold hammer above the egg.) "What would happen to this egg if I hit it with a hammer? [Allow students to answer.] Now I'll place this egg under the pot to stand for the Christian's being 'hidden with Christ in God'. No matter how weak a Christian he may be, when he belongs to Christ he is perfectly safe.

"Let's see how safe he is. Suppose the devil tempts him-just a little. (*Teacher:* Tap the pot with the hammer.) Does that hurt the egg? Suppose he hits harder. Does that touch the egg? What if Satan pounds and pounds? Does the egg break? (*Teacher:* Hit the pot harder each time.) No? Why not? Because the egg is as safe as the pot is. And when your life is 'hid with Christ in God,' you are exactly as safe as Christ is. Since He can take any blow that may come, you will never lose your salvation. It makes no difference how weak you are, for He is strong.

"If you're trusting the Lord as your Saviour, you are perfectly safe from any attack on your salvation. Because your salvation is perfect, no one can add a thing to it. Keeping old Jewish laws, worshiping angels, punishing one's self—none of these are needed to save us or to keep us saved. When our trust is in Christ alone, we are saved and safe forever."

Show Illustration #11

Archippus looked lovingly at his family. "So," he said, "no matter where we are—here at home, down at the market, or anywhere else—Satan cannot take away our salvation. We are forever joined to Christ, our living Head, and we are hidden with Him in God." (See 1 Corinthians 3:23.)

4. WHEN CHRIST REIGNS ON EARTH, HIS BODY OF BELIEVERS WILL REIGN WITH HIM
Colossians 3:4

Then, drawing four arrows on a piece of paper, Archippus explained: "We cannot see the Lord Jesus now, even though He is in us and with us always. A day is coming, however, when our eyes shall see Him. Then wherever He is, we shall be. These arrows will help you understand."

Show Illustration #12a

"The Lord Jesus came down to earth (*Teacher:* point to first arrow), lived, died for our sins, and rose from the dead.

Show Illustration 12b

Later He went back to Heaven and is now sitting alongside God the Father. (See Hebrews 10:12.) Some day, we don't know when—it could be today!

Show Illustration 12c

He'll come back in the air and catch up to Heaven all whose trust is in Him, both the living and the dead. From that moment on, we His body and He our Head, shall be together forever,

Show Illustration 12d

Seven years later we shall come with Him to earth (fourth arrow) for 1,000 years. (See Revelation 20:4.)

Show Illustration #12e

"Here on earth He, the King of kings and Lord of lords, shall reign and we with Him." (See Revelation 5:10; 19:16; 20:4-6.)

The children clapped their hands and jumped up and down, crying, "Do you mean it, Daddy? We'll go up to Heaven with the Lord Jesus and then come back to earth with Him? Is it just a story? Or is it really true?"

"It is true—absolutely true. Here, read it for yourself: 'When Christ . . . appears, then will you also appear with Him in glory. His glory—His shining brightness—will be ours. We shall be like Him. (See 1 John 3:2.) Imagine that! Until then we can—and should—serve Him. By doing loving, helpful things for our families, our friends, our church, we thank Him for His wonderful salvation."

Before we pray, will you list in your notebook some acts of love which you can do today? This week? Then, when we do these things, we shall be pleasing God and thanking Him for our Saviour.

Lesson 4
CHRIST FIRST

> **NOTE TO THE TEACHER**
>
> You are God's instrument to give His Word to your students. He wants you to teach so that they will understand and obey it.
>
> How do you prepare your lesson? Do you start with prayer, asking God to guide you? Do you study the Scripture so thoroughly that you know it? As you study, do you keep the aim of the lesson in your mind? Is your life affected by the lesson? In connection with this particular study, are you giving the Lord Jesus Christ first place in every area of your own life?
>
> You have doubtless observed the similarities between the Ephesian and Colossian letters. In Ephesians, the emphasis is on the Church, the body of which Christ is the Head. In Colossians, the emphasis is on Christ, the Head of the body which is the Church.
>
> Paul begins Ephesians by showing what Christ did for believers. (They were chosen, placed as sons, accepted, redeemed, and sealed by Him.) In the last part of the letter, Paul taught believers how they should obey Christ in everyday situations.
>
> Throughout the Colossian letter, Paul shows that Christ is head high over all. Believers are therefore urged to do what God has done: put Christ first. Near the end of the letter, he reveals how practical this truth is in every part of life.

Scripture to be studied: Colossians 3:5-4:6

The *aim* of the lesson: *To show that in every part of life, we are to put Christ first.*

What your students should *know*: The Christian has his greatest happiness when he gives Christ first place.

What your students should *feel*: Hatred for anything that would push Christ out of His rightful first place.

What your students should *do*: Turn from sinful habits, and determine what they can do to live Christ-like lives.

Lesson outline (for the teacher's and students' notebooks):

1. The believer's responsibility to himself (3:5-11).
2. The believer's responsibility to other believers (3:12-17).
3. The believer's responsibility at home and work (3:18-4:1).
4. The believer's responsibility to God (4:2-6).

The verse to be memorized:

That in all things Christ might have the preeminence.
(Colossians 1:18b)

THE LESSON

The people who lived in Bible times were much like us. Their clothing may have been quite different. Their houses were not like ours. But there were fathers who worked. Some were farmers; others were carpenters; many were fishermen. The mothers washed clothes and prepared meals. The children helped with the work at home, carried water and played games. Have you ever wished that some of those people could come back to life? Do you have a good imagination? Let us suppose that Mr. and Mrs. Philemon, their children and one of their slaves were right here, eager to tell us what happened long ago.

"As you know, the church in Colosse met in our home," Mr. Philemon begins. "Several in our city had trusted in the Lord Jesus Christ. We had no New Testament, for it was just being written at that time. Because we knew so little about the Christian life, we made mistakes. For example, when teachers came along with new ideas, we accepted them, Some of our people started worshiping angels. They studied the old Jewish law and observed Jewish holy days, even though they weren't Jews. They denied themselves certain good things. They thought this self-punishment would make them worthy of salvation, or at least more holy and sure of going to Heaven.

"But God had His eye on us. He knew we truly wanted to do right. So He caused the Apostle Paul to write us a letter. Paul was a prisoner far away in Rome. Most of our people had never seen him. So it was a great day for us when we heard from him. After the letter was read, we discussed each part of it, sometimes at church, other times in our homes. Through that letter the Holy Spirit taught us that the Lord Jesus Christ is high over all. He is Head of the universe because He created everything. He is the Head of the church because He bought it with His precious blood. We who are believers are His body and are joined to him, the Head. So His life is ours. We are complete. We have all we need for this life and the next. So we Colossians got rid of the false ideas which the so-called 'wise' teachers had taught us. We gave Christ His right place."

Mrs. Philemon adds quietly, "Yes, but be sure to tell them *how* we put Christ first."

"That was an important part of Paul's letter to us," Mr. Philemon declares. "After that section (3:5-4:6) was read to us, we divided into groups to talk it over. My wife was with the women; the children were together and the men gathered up front. We passed Paul's letter from one to the other."

1. THE BELIEVER'S RESPONSIBILITY TO HIMSELF
Colossians 3:5-11

Show Illustration #13a

"We men were upset because the Holy Spirit named some terrible sins: sex sins, dirty-mindedness, wanting what belongs to others. These are selfish sins–all of them. A person who practices them is interested only in himself and His own pleasure. It's as if he is carrying a sign announcing: *Me First*. We were all like that before we placed our trust in the Saviour. Apparently there were some in our number who were still like that. 'Put those things to death,' the Holy Spirit commanded. 'It is for these very sins that the anger of God comes down on those who refuse to obey Him.'

– 25 –

Show illustration #13b

"God's Spirit listed other things we were to get rid of: anger, bad temper, evil thoughts about others, speaking against God, filthy talk, lies. One after another, we hung our heads in shame. We had been easy on ourselves. There were times when I got angry at my children for making noise. So I'd go into a rage, shouting at them and making more noise than they did! Sometimes my wife wanted me to fix something. In a fit of temper I'd exclaim, 'Fix it yourself! I'm tired!' I would rather not tell you how many lies I've told. If telling the truth would embarrass me before others, I'd just tell a lie to make myself look good, even though I was a Christian.

"The day the Colossian letter was read we silently confessed our sins to God. We admitted we had been putting ourselves first. Earnestly we promised that, with His help, Christ would be first in our daily living. It has not always been easy. I've often been tempted to please myself. There have been times I have yielded to the temptation, I'm sorry to say. But each day I ask God to help me put *Christ First*. And He does help me more and more."

2. THE BELIEVER'S RESPONSIBILITY TO OTHER BELIEVERS
Colossians 3:2-17

Mrs. Philemon speaks up. "That day while the men were re-reading the letter and praying, we ladies were talking about our own selfishness. According to the custom of our day, women stayed at home most of the time. It wasn't so hard for me, for my husband was a successful businessman and we had a nice home. I was proud of our home. I was proud that we had slaves to do much of the work. Because I felt we were better than others, I was harsh and unkind. If I quarreled with someone, I refused to forgive that person. I, I, I. That's the one I thought about all the time. Me first! Others were much like me, unfortunately. And we were miserable. Our hearts were pricked when we heard, 'Your new life should be filled with sympathy for others. Show kindness. Don't allow yourself to be proud. Put up with one another. Forgive those who wrong you or hurt you. Christ has forgiven you, so you must be willing to forgive others. Be loving, for love holds everything and everybody together.' Christ would certainly have first place in our actions if we followed these instructions."

Mrs. Philemon continues, "Paul's letter included three commands: (*Teacher:* Your students should write these in their notebooks.)

1. Let Christ's teaching (and His Word) live in you in full measure.
2. In wisdom, teach others and help them.
3. Sing Christian songs, praising God with thankful hearts.

Show Illustration #14

"We women were especially glad for these orders. We could study God's Word every day. We could teach it to our children and share it with other ladies. We could thank God for His blessings by singing songs of praise to Him. The children also could learn to sing God's praises. All of these could be practiced in our homes. And by so doing, Christ would be first in our thoughts and words."

3. THE BELIEVER'S RESPONSIBILITY AT HOME AND WORK
Colossians 3:18-4:1

Mr. Philemon adds, "Things in Colosse 1900 years ago (when Paul wrote this letter) were quite different from today. Wives, children and servants were not given any consideration. Servants worked hard but were rarely paid, for most of them were slaves. And wives and children were usually treated like slaves. However, the instructions which God gave to families changed our way of living completely."

Mrs. Philemon admits, "I had never respected my husband. I wanted my own way. But then I learned that I was to yield myself to him and obey him because this was what God wanted. When I did what God wanted me to do, He made me happier than I had ever been! Not only that, I came to respect my husband and love him deeply."

Mr. Philemon smiles at his wife, saying, "God gets all the credit for that. For at the same time He taught me that I was to love you and treat you kindly–no matter how unkind you might be to me."

One of Philemon's sons clears his throat. "And we learned that it pleased the Lord when we obeyed our parents," he says. "So from then on it was easier to do what they said. It was our way of putting Christ first in our lives."

Show Illustration #15

Mr. Philemon declares, "From the early part of the letter to the Colossians we learned that Christ is Head over the universe and Head over the Church. As He is the Head over the Church, so the husband is the head over the wife. (See Ephesians 5:23.) Together they are tools in the hands of the Lord–tools that shape the lives of their children. So when children obey their parents, and the wife obeys her husband, and the husband loves his wife, they are all putting Christ first. And that is as it should be, because the Lord Jesus is also the Head of the family."

"May I add something?" the slave asks. "Before Paul's letter came, I obeyed Mr. Philemon because I had to. Disobedient slaves could be put to death. The Holy Spirit taught me that I was not to do my work simply to please a man. I was to work for him just as if I were working for God. I was to put my heart in it, for when I served Mr. Philemon I was really serving the Lord Christ. He is the One who allowed me to be a slave. So I served my heavenly Father by serving my earthly master well. In this way I was putting Christ first. And I will get a reward in Heaven. Think of that!"

Mr. Philemon adds, "It was a sober truth that was given to us who were masters of slaves. We were commanded to treat them fairly and as equals. That was hard to do at first. But by remembering that we who are earthly masters have a Master in Heaven, we want to treat them as He treats us. By accepting slaves as our equals, we are putting Christ first."

4. THE BELIEVER'S RESPONSIBILITY TO GOD
Colossians 4:2-6

Mr. Philemon has something more to say, "When we get rid of old sinful habits, putting them out of our lives completely, we give Christ first place. By studying God's Word and sharing it with others, and by singing songs of praise to God, we give Christ the first place. If we accept our right place in our family and in our work, we are giving Christ His place."

Show Illustration #16a

"Two other commands were given in the Colossian letter," Mr. Philemon continues. "We are to cling to God in prayer and thanksgiving. Like the Lord Jesus, we should have specific times for prayer. It may be in the early morning, or perhaps late into the night. In addition, we should talk to our heavenly Father all through the day, asking Him to guide us. Prayer guards the Christian against the devil. Prayer helps the Christian to win other souls for the Lord Jesus.

Show Illustration #16b

"After we pray–even while we're praying–we are to work. We're commanded to use care and be wise so the unsaved will see that we are Christ-like. Then they'll want to listen to us when we tell them about the Saviour who loves them. It is our responsibility to take advantage of every opportunity that God gives us, speaking His message graciously.

"When our lives are controlled by prayer and our lips are filled with God's message of salvation, Christ truly has first place in our lives."

These truths which the Philemon family learned long ago are also for us today. Are you willing to give the Lord Jesus the highest place in your life? If so, please list in your notebook the things you plan to do this moment, this week:

1. Sinful habits you are getting rid of.
2. Clean new habits you want to practice.
3. Rules you want to follow at home and at work.
4. Your requests for prayer.
5. Your purpose to share the Gospel with others.

(***Teacher:*** Pray aloud for your students who are making decisions that will affect their lives here on earth–and in Heaven. If you have unsaved students present, give them opportunity to give Christ His rightful place as Saviour.)

www.ingramcontent.com/pod-product-compliance
Lightning Source LLC
Chambersburg PA
CBHW060803090426
42736CB00002B/135